THE TEN PRISON COMMANDMENTS

JOHN "DOC" FULLER

THE TEN PRISON COMMANDMENTS

**Ten Rules You Must Know Before You
Enter a County Jail, State or Federal Prison**

JOHN "DOC" FULLER

Table of Contents

INTRODUCTION

If you are a young person in school, a professional athlete, a celebrity, or a hard-working person contemplating or engaging in criminal acts, you should seek help from a family member, guidance counselor, teacher, spiritual advisor, true friend, mentor, or qualified mental health professional. Then you may never have to enter the prison system and apply the commandments I've outlined in this book.

You'll also get to avoid those who choose to be sneaky, perverted, selfish, haughty, greedy, and violent. Unlike you, these individuals could not be talked out of their deviant behavior, and so they are languishing in our nation's numerous penal institutions just waiting for someone like you to stumble in and violate their unwritten rules, providing an easy target for their rage. Please do not take this warning lightly.

Combined, the author has spent over 11 years in various prisons throughout the country, so he knows all too well of what he speaks.

Perhaps you're already in prison. If so, you may have an opportunity to exit prison one day and re-establish yourself as an honorable person in society. Right now, you may think that's impossible. But if I can do it, so can you. However, the only way you'll survive to see that day is if you learn and obey the commandments outlined in this book.

The Ten Prison Commandments are based upon my extensive experience in high, medium, and low security institutions around the country. I am saddened by the unnecessary tragedies that occur in these facilities each day. They motivated me to write this book on the most important "don'ts" when it comes to surviving prison. I sincerely hope that you will never need to apply these commandments. However, the grim reality is that some people will.

Implementing these commandments can possibly save your life, but only if you are willing to abandon the belief that you are tougher, wealthier, smarter, or more privileged than your fellow inmates.

This short publication covers a lot of ground, but it will not cover every scenario you may face in prison. Why? Simply put the environment inside jails and prisons vary according to their security levels. The culture of the inmates who have an influence in these facilities and the staff members who run them will also differ. But once you get a grasp for the basic rules by which prison culture operates, you should be able to adapt these commandments as needed.

The rules in this book address the primary causes of violence in the inmate subculture resulting from a process called "Institutionalization."

Institutionalization occurs when one adapts to and depends on the laws or unwritten rules within a structured or well-established system. Life in prison often causes inmates to consciously or unconsciously relinquish their independence and responsibility.

If you are not conscious of offending others while adjusting to the often cold, unbending prison routine that deprives you of privacy and freedom, you can easily succumb to violence. This can be avoided if you know some basic principles that apply regardless of the setting or culture.

Don't be fooled: You can be seriously injured or killed for breaking a rule you didn't know existed. A breach of unwritten prison rules will anger not only correctional officers but inmates as well.

Quite frankly, correctional officers do want to complete a report about inmate assaults or assign another inmate to clean up your blood, urine, or fecal matter after an attack. Ignorance is no defense. Information is power.

In some instances a family member or friend may bring you to self-surrender to prison.

Others are arrested at their home, workplace or scene of the crime. After sitting in their local county jail for months, they are sentenced and transported by US Marshalls or state prison officials to their new "home away from home." No matter how you got to workplace or scene of the crime. After sitting in their local county jail for months, they are sentenced and transported by US Marshalls or state prison officials to their new "home away from home." No matter how you got to prison, this publication will provide you with an advantage over others who arrive with you.

Most if not all who enter the prison systems do so out of arrogance, greed, and the inability to appreciate what they have in life. Shady CEOs, deceitful stockbrokers, dishonest politicians, snobbish entertainers, dishonorable bankers, unethical attorneys, spoiled professional and college athletes, disgusting rapists, murders and the hoodlum street corner drug dealer all share the belief that they will never get caught. Those who can afford a high-powered attorney do not believe they will be found guilty.

Rich criminals leave behind a few cherished Picassos, Lichtensteins, Lamborghini Sesto Elementos, McLarens, Zenvos, Franck Mullers, Piagets, Vacheron Constantins, George Steck Pianos, and several homes. Middle class criminals leave behind the Lexus, Corvette, Rolex, Versace eyewear, time-shares and one or two homes. Street level hustlers leave behind their .9 millimeters, small bags of marijuana, PS3's, Xbox's, video games, several pairs of sneakers, fitted baseball caps, hooded sweatshirts and one or two cell phones.

The street level hustlers were snubbed by the rich and most middle class as they pulled their luxury cars into gated communities filled with beautiful Travertine driveways, well-trimmed hedges, and breathtaking flowerbeds. However, in prison, it's the street level criminals who are respected, feared, and admired as their thirst for confrontation, intimidation, and violence permeates the air.

Your navigation within prison walls will become manageable if you apply these commandments. They are beneficial to the U.S. Citizen, Non U.S. Citizen, educated, uneducated, black, white, young, old, rich, or poor. Take advantage of this knowledge whether you are designated to a county jail or high security prison. With that being said, let's get into the commandments.

COMMANDMENT 1:
DO NOT STARE AT OTHER INMATES

Inmates will stare at you and size you up when you arrive. Do not return the favor. They know you are new to the joint, because they will see you carrying your bedroll or fish kit, (blanket, sheet and pillowcase rolled up) to your cell or dorm with a nervous look that indicates you are scared, sad, or intimidated about your new environment.

The atmosphere will likely be loud. Most inmates will be playing cards, trash talking, or watching television. You will feel the need to look at other inmates as you walk into your designated area. However, do not hold your stare for more than a second or two. Otherwise inmates may interpret it as a challenge that you intend to assert dominance over them. Your stare could also be misconstrued as anger and thrust you into an immediate state of disapproval.

One after another, inmates will put you on their hit list and take action as a result of your seemingly innocent stare.

Others may take your stare to mean you are interested in them sexually. Unless you are looking for that kind of attention, I suggest you look away. If it was common for you to hold a stare to intimidate others in the workplace, at school, or other environments, you should kick the habit immediately.

In prison, staring is nothing more than an invitation to violence.

COMMANDMENT 2:
DO NOT TRUST YOUR FELLOW INMATES

Most people regard prisoners as lowlife thieves, murderers, drug dealers, and white-collar con artists who cannot be trusted or rehabilitated. For the most part, they are right. Prison is a jungle full of nothing but predators. This means the first person who tries to help you will likely have an ulterior motive. You will be in a vulnerable state emotionally. After all, you've left your family, friends, and trusted associates behind. You are the equivalent of a newborn, because you have no experience in your new environment, and there's absolutely no one you can trust. Seasoned inmates recognize this, and they will be quick to exploit your weaknesses.

You will probably be asked questions such as "Where are you from?" "How much time do you have?" Or "What are you in prison for?" Then you will likely hear the infamous follow-up questions: "Do you want some snacks, deodorant, shampoo, sneakers, or stamps?"

Your answer to each of these questions should be a firm "No." The only exception you might want to make on the first day in prison is using shower shoes. Prison showers contain semen, germs, and fungus. The last thing you need when embarking on your new life in prison is a skin infection on your feet. Inmates customarily offer shower shoes to new fellow prisoners. There is a general consensus in prison that no one wants to begin his incarceration by picking up a nasty foot infection. Your other alternative is to use the cheap, low cut orange or blue sneakers they issue inmates when processed into the institution.

Some prisoners are looking for a way out. If you think revealing your involvement in some elaborate but unsolved Ponzi scheme, inside trade, murder, or drug deal you pulled off is the way to endear yourself to other inmates, think again. It's flat out stupid and reckless to brag or divulge information about unsolved crimes you committed on the outside. Your fellow inmates will leap at the opportunity to help federal or state authorities solve the crime in the hope that doing so will reduce their own sentence. Prisons are flooded with a new breed of criminals who are flat out weak. Real gangsters and stand up guys are as rare as an eclipse. Inmates can also be wired as confidential informants.

In addition, do not be fooled by those who want to introduce you to their female friends, who will write, visit, or bring drugs into prison for you. They will turn your two-year term into a life sentence by involving you in schemes to smuggle drugs and other contraband into prison. If you have a wife by your side, please respect her. She is all you need!

Most inmates do not have money, so they will be very interested to see what you can afford once money is posted to your account. Then they will see how they can use your money against you. Some inmates will merely want to borrow items you have purchased or have you purchase items for them from the commissary. Others will extort your money from you or force you to join their gang.

It is wise to wait months before opening up to anyone, but even then, do not trust anyone completely. Remember: Even your most trusted confidante was someone else's friend before he met you, so don't think your personal business will not be leaked out and used against you at some point. Assume the worst of everyone.

If you simply exercise patience and pay attention to what is going on around you, it is easy to spot inmates with quick tempers and bad character. It will also be easy to hear the gossip and watch prison schemes unfold. If you see trouble brewing, go to another area immediately.

Likely, the trouble is related to gang conflict, a bad debt, or lack of respect. If you are hanging with guys who are gang banging, drinking, drugging, gambling, or smoking you will suffer the consequences for those bad choices.

Sex Offenders

Pedophiles, rapists and sexual predators please read this several times.

Keep your mouths quiet because inmates will find out who you are sooner or later. The wheels of justice turn very slow for you sick vermin. There will come a time when you are exposed. Once that happens you will feel what your victim(s) felt. All dignity will be lost and cries for help ignored. The courts rarely make trash like you pay the full price for the heinous acts you commit but don't worry, inmates happily pick up the tab. Ironically they may lift your head like the predator if given enough time to trap you one on one. Will you deserve it? Probably so but if you're honest the question should be "Did my victim(s) deserve to be physically, emotionally, psychologically or verbally abused?"

COMMANDMENT 3:
RESPECT YOUR CELLMATE

In the Cell

Now that you've walked through the dorm to your designated cell, your bunky (cellmate) may be there reading, writing, or sleeping. Do not be shocked if his underwear are hanging on a makeshift clothesline (portion of torn bed sheet usually ½ thick) or his pictures and artwork are stuck to the wall with toothpaste (prisons multipurpose glue). This was his home prior to your arrival, so do not comment or ask questions about his personal belongings. Refrain from inquiring why he is in prison, when he is getting out, or where he is from. He may provide that information when he feels comfortable with you.

Respect your cellmate's property. Do not take it upon yourself to read his personal mail, magazines, or newspapers. Don't even think about eating his food. Your cellmate may not have much, so do not bother the little he has. Of course, insist that he give you the same respect once you are able to purchase items of your own.

In the Restroom

If you are in a facility where inmates are locked down 23 hours per day and must use the cell toilet, let your cellmate know before you go. If he is on the bottom bunk, he will likely put up a sheet so you can have privacy. Otherwise, use your own sheet. Simply tuck it under your mattress if you have the top bunk—or under his mattress if you don't. But ask permission first! This is delicate but essential. Your bunky should turn his back, and you had better flush the toilet immediately and often to avoid smelling up the cell.

If the restrooms are in an open-style setting, flush immediately even if all you do is pass gas. Your bunky is not one of your fart buddies from high school. He will feel disrespected and may try to kill you while you are on the toilet with your pants down.

Do your utmost to respect other inmates' hygiene time. Using the toilet is something that cannot be avoided, but it can be done with respect. You may get a warning the first time, but if you take your sweet time flushing or fail to flush at all, you will without doubt suffer the consequences.

Inmate Names

Respect others by using their preferred name. If an inmate is called "Leftover Louie," "Old Head," or "Money Mike," by all means use that name. More than likely he has earned it in prison or has carried the name since childhood. If an open homosexual uses a name like

"Michelle," "Cherry," or "Cindy," respectfully use their name of choice. They may look feminine, but they are still men, and they will transform into fighting machines right before your eyes if you decide to call them by the name on their birth certificate or government ID. That's why some refer to homosexuals as "Transformers." If you come from a neighborhood where it's common to call your friends "gay," "punk," "faggots," or the "B-word," stop it. It is the quickest death sentence you could inflict upon yourself. Those words immediately categorize someone as gay, homosexual, or soft (incapable of holding his own). In essence, you are saying, "You are not a man. You are a woman who engages in anal and oral sex. I can strong-arm you and take your belongings or your manhood if I choose, and that's a fact."

If other inmates see you refer to another man as a faggot, punk, or "B," they will expect him to harm you. Most inmates frown upon homosexuality, and reputations are protected at all costs.

Although men who are not homophobic often have their hair braided by homosexuals, they never do so behind closed doors. Consensual hair braiding in a wide-open area clearly demonstrates nothing other than hair braiding is taking place, so an inmate's reputation is protected. If you are a homosexual, the wisest course of action is to keep it to yourself while in prison, because it will only cause you problems. Some prisons have gay cellblocks to prevent homosexuals from being harassed, raped, or killed out of spite.

COMMANDMENT 4:
MIND YOUR BUSINESS

Watching Television

Respect must also be shown in the television room. Never change the channel without permission. That's a suicide mission. Inmates work out their television viewing schedules days, weeks, seasons, even years ahead of time. It is their lifeline to the outside world, a way of numbing the pain of prison life, so they will defend it at all costs. Sports rule the television room in prison. Even corrections officers are leery of interfering with sports programs.

Normally prisons will shut televisions off between 10:00 p.m. and 11:30 p.m. Those hours are extended for events such as the Super Bowl, World Cup Soccer, NBA finals, World Series and championship boxing if the facility is equipped with cable.

Inmates have self-designated spaces where their chairs are placed inside TV rooms. If you are assigned or provided a chair and bring it inside the television room, do not be surprised if someone asks you to move, particularly if your seat is close to the television or placed where you can get a good view. You will literally be sitting in "their spot." Your safest bet is to ask if a certain area on the floor belongs to anyone else prior to setting down your chair.

You will earn the right to a better spot on the floor as inmates transfer out of your housing unit. It may take months or years depending on the average length of time inmates spend in your unit. Higher security prisons will dictate the seriousness of your intended or unintended disrespect in the television room. Please become a respectful viewer in the television room to avoid unnecessary consequences.

In the Cafeteria

Disrespect in the cafeteria can be deadly. Numerous situations can literally get you murdered before you digest your first meal. Unlike the impolite world outside of prison where family and friends allow you to hop in front of them to avoid long lines at movie theatres, supermarkets, restaurants, or sporting venues, if you try this in prison, you're a dead man. In prison, you line up for everything—the commissary, telephone, picking up or dropping off laundry, and waiting to see your counselor or case manager. Few line-cutting confrontations occur outside of prison, because most people do not wish to argue or fight in public. Instead patrons quietly whisper and gape at the blatant disrespect. Persons waiting in line may also tolerate line-cutting because of celebrity status or because you have clout with the owner of the establishment. That clout means nothing in prison. Respect is the currency of prison society.

Most of the inmates you cut in front of will look to pay you a nasty visit before the night is over.

Respect your race by sitting at a table with people your color first, ethnicity second. The higher the security level at your facility, the more important this is. If you're Caucasian, scour the room like the Terminator while waiting in line to see where other white people are sitting. If your housing unit has been called to eat first, it may be difficult to ascertain where your race sits. If you are an African American inmate, watch where other African American inmates in your unit take their seat. As with the television room, races have established boundaries inside the cafeteria. If you are white and realize black men or other ethnicities are beginning to sit at your table or in the surrounding area, knock once on the table (that's right, knock), get up, and leave. Knocking is a sign of respect and a way of respectfully saying goodbye without talking.

If you are big and black and think you can handle the 85-pound white boy at the table and refuse to knock or respectfully acknowledge that you are leaving the table, guess again. You've just disrespected every other white person who sits in that section the cafeteria. Cafeterias are part of the prison jungle where territories are clearly marked. It's the figurative waterhole where inmates come to eat and drink. Learn from the lions, elephants, hyenas and wilder beast on television and stick within the boundaries of your pride.

If cutting in line is the first thing that results in violence in prison cafeterias, reaching across tables is probably second.

You are not in a McDonalds, your place of employment nor a hospital cafeteria where reaching, grabbing or taking condiments at an occupied table are acceptable. Even when sitting with people within your race, if you see packets of sugar, salt, or pepper on the table prior to your arrival, respectfully ask, "Is it okay to take one?" Reaching across another inmate's tray is likewise blatantly disrespectful. Inmates do not generally wait until you leave the cafeteria to settle these matters. They are handled instantly. And because you will be assaulted swiftly, you will not stand a chance. The assault will happen as fast as it took to reach across the table without asking permission for the condiment. No one will assist you for that type of disrespect.

In the Weight Room

The weight room remains the primary outlet for inmates who want to get the aggression out of their system. Initially, you may find it difficult to establish a workout routine, because everyone is using the weights. Do not become frustrated or lose your cool. Inmates have established workout routines with the same weightlifting partners for years. Their gym schedules are planned days, weeks or months ahead of time. The dumbbells and steel plates are shared regularly with the men they have seen in the gym at the same time for months and years. They reciprocate favors to one another so that their time in the gym is unimpeded.

If you decide to get in shape and start lifting weights, ask permission to take weights if they are not sitting on the rack. The worst time to be disrespectful is in the gym where testosterone is at its peak. Losing your cool will get you tossed around like a rag doll or hit in the head with a dumbbell or steel plate. Over time, inmates will adjust to seeing you in the gym. They will see your level of respect and determine how serious you are about staying in shape. Only then will they go out of their way to ask you "Would you like these weights when we are finished?" You should cherish those words.

COMMANDMENT 5:
RESPECT THE STAFF

Corrections officers are hired to do a job, and for the most part they will not cause trouble intentionally. There is a chance along your prison stay that prison staff you may be asked to perform a task outside of your work duties. For instance, an officer in your housing unit may ask you to pick up a piece of paper and throw it in the garbage. The request might be made out of spite. Even so, simply pick it up and toss in the trash. Failure to throw the paper in the garbage will result in a written sanction for "Refusing to obey a direct order." Furthermore, word of your disobedience could spread to other staff members, making your life inside more miserable then it already is. Officers who work the shift after the incident may toss items around in your locker, delay informing you that your visit has arrived, hold your mail longer than necessary, or look for other opportunities to make you frustrated, angry, and resentful.

Chances are high that others within the institution know the correctional officer in question is a flat out nutcase. However, you are an inmate, which means you are expected to follow instructions whether reasonable or unreasonable. These behaviors occur more often in lower security prisons, because the mentality of the officers reflects the ill-mannered society outside of prison. Staff members in your correctional institution are supposed to be united. However, senseless correctional officers slip through the cracks sometimes, as do greedy stockbrokers, corrupt police officers, immoral teachers, evil doctors, and depraved coaches in the world you chose to leave behind.

COMMANDMENT 6:
DO NOT STEAL

Inmate lockers containing personal items may be wide open if inmates are in the vicinity. Even so, do not stare into cubicles, cells, or other areas that contain personal property. Generally, lockers in higher security prisons are also left wide open while inmates are in another part of the prison. Why? Prisons run according to respectful and even remarkable laws when it comes to stealing that regular society does not. Outside of prison, disrespect for the property of others prevalent. Thieves will not hesitate to break into your car or home and steal your property. A thief can destroy your vehicle merely because he or she wants a purse, cigarettes, or a cell phone. Even in places of employment, classified information, computers, purses, and other personal items are stolen. If such actions were met immediately with physical punishment, as they are in prison, such situations would not occur nearly as often.

In high and medium security prisons, court is held instantly, with dire consequences. As such, coveting other people's personal items is curbed at all times. In lower security prisons, stealing happens more often. Why? Because people are closer to being released, and the low standards of outside society are already beginning to seep back in. As such, thieves are more prevalent in low security institutions and prison camps.

Never forget that some inmates in low security levels and camps have worked their way "down" from higher security prisons over the years. When it comes to dealing with thieves, their mentality has not changed. Most will sacrifice their release date in order to inflict bodily harm upon a thief. Thieves in prison are universally detested like rats and roaches so don't put yourself in a position to get squashed—or exterminated.

As dangerous as it is to steal from fellow inmates, it is acceptable to steal from prison staff members, because it's deemed, "Having one up on The Man." To steal a counselor's wrist watch, hat, or keys is to steal from the state or the government. In no way am I suggesting that you steal from correctional officers. To steal from anyone while you are in prison only reinforces the fact that you deserve to be there. My point is that you should not be surprised if you see it occur with the approval of other inmates. If you are a thief on any level, call it quits or your life will be in jeopardy and deservedly so.

Come to prison with cash so you can purchase necessary items as quickly as possible. Then you will not be tempted to steal. Most correctional facilities will also encourage you to purchase a lock from commissary to store food, photos, hygiene products, legal papers, etc. Even though theft is discouraged in prison, it is still better to purchase a lock so as not to tempt your fellow inmates.

COMMANDMENT 7:
DON'T BE A SNITCH

One of the best things you can do in prison is to see and hear everything going on in your immediate environment and yet say nothing. Correctional officers may ask you for information about an incident involving other inmates or confiscated contraband. Simply claim that you were looking the other way and didn't see or hear anything. While this may irritate the staff, they will likely understand your need for self-preservation.

Avoid talking to guards in a friendly way or being seen inside their office, because other prisoners will assume you are snitching. Even a conversation about sports can be construed as snitching. Keep in mind that if you are a high profile case, such as Bernie Madoff, inmates have watched the news and will be aware that you cooperated with the authorities. Bernie was not a snitch.

However, inmates did not care for him because he ruined the lives of so many hard working people. So do not parade around as if you are a standup guy knowing you are an informant, rat, snake or better yet a blazing hot snitch. They will never trust you for snitching, and those who associate with you will have an ulterior motive. After all, why would anyone in prison want to associate with a snitch? It would make more sense to swallow a Bengay and Ajax sandwich than to be friends with a snitch.

COMMANDMENT 8:
AVOID PRISON GANGS

Most inmates do not need to join a gang for protection. Their crimes involved some type of infraction that was not gang related, such as fraud, drug dealing, murder, credit card schemes, mortgage scams, kidnapping, child molestation, or Ponzi schemes. Those who join gangs are likely scared or decided to find a family they did not believed existed. Either that or they were violent prior to prison and, as such, absolutely, have to join a gang for survival.

If you find yourself in a high security prison, do your best to avoid joining a gang. The majority of prison violence emanates from gang retaliation against their rivals. You don't want to get caught in the middle of such conflicts.

Even though most gangs are divided along racial lines, being loyal to your race does not mean you have to join a gang. The primary gangs that reign in prison are: the Bloods, Crips, the Aryan Brotherhood, MS 13, La Familia Nuestra, the Black Guerilla Family, Texas Syndicate, and the Mexican Mafia.

Some gangs have a "blood in/blood out" rule, which means they must kill someone to get in and die to get out. If you join a gang, there is a good chance you will not go home on time, because you will be involved in illegal activities that often include violence against other inmates. Your gang will be your family, and family comes first. Throw common sense out the window. Failure to follow orders will result in punishment. If a fellow gang member is attacked, you are expected to help them. That means you will likely get hurt or killed.

Keep in mind that if you decide to join a gang, you will likely be in it for the rest of your life. In some instances, when gang members leave prison they are given only a few days to contact a higher ranking gang member. If you don't, you and your family may be severely beaten or killed. If you are in a gang that does not practice the blood in/blood out rule, get out while you can. Then your family will not have to suffer the consequences of you being involved in that lifestyle.

Prison is not the place to learn violence. Prison gangs take pride in being physically prepared for extreme violence unlike some (not all) fake gangbangers on the street who don't work out, wear saggy pants, impregnate young misguided women, smoke weed, sell crack to buy a pair of sneakers, and play violent video games all day. Those distractions do not exist in prison. Furthermore, prison gangs don't play at being tough. They're the toughest—and most dangerous—people you'll ever meet.

COMMANDMENT 9:
STAY AWAY FROM DRUGS

If you are foolish enough to use drugs while in prison, you are embarking on a hasty trip to self-inflicted pain and suffering. If a corrections officer catches you with drugs, you may face outside charges in addition to the cancelation of phone privileges and visits. They will rightfully assume that a friend or family member smuggled them into prison for you, particularly if you receive frequent visits.

The street value of drugs multiplies exponentially in prison, which means you are also going to break the bank.

Penitentiaries are a slower version of the Internet. Plenty of officers will take $500 to provide your location, but well-connected inmates never need an officer for such information. They simply send your name out to several friends in various institutions. Those friends send the message to their friends and so on. It is like putting your physical well-being on layaway.

Apart from drug debts, drugs like heroin and cocaine may cause you to overdose immediately, particularly if you've been drug-free for months or years. As a prison consultant, I always encourage individuals who are self-surrendering to ensure they are drug and alcohol-free prior to self-surrendering. You may be able to pay a drug tab for the first few weeks, but keep in mind that the economic circumstances of families change dramatically over time, especially if you were the primary breadwinner. Officers are also rotated to other housing units, causing smuggling operations to cease at a moment's notice. Your drug connect can also get busted. If he is facing serious time for possessing drugs while in prison, he might dime you out, particularly if he is scheduled to be released in the near future.

COMMANDMENT 10:
DO NOT GAMBLE

Travel the world, and it's unlikely you will find a population of individuals who love to gamble more than inmates. Most prison violence stems from gambling debts. Are you a candidate? Yes. Why? Consider the fact that an impulsive behavior of some sort landed you in prison in the first place. Your thrill for the "quick fix," desire to pass time, have an adrenaline rush, or fit in with other inmates will lead to gambling in some fashion. I am not a sociologist, but I firmly believe there is a high correlation between committing crimes and gambling. After all, didn't you gamble on getting away with the crime that landed you in prison in the first place?

Do not gamble even if you belong to a gang. If you think your gang will protect you simply because you lost a bet and refuse to pay other gang members or races, I have a news flash for you: Your fellow gang members may actually be the ones held responsible for punishing you. It is not uncommon for gangs to beat their fellow members severely with a lock inside a sock due to such foolishness. As I stated in Commandment 4, the gang's obligation is to protect you. However, your failure to pay can lead to a tremendous gang or race riot. Severely thrashing you will keep overall violence down and prevent rival gangs and races from serious wounds that are generally reserved for other gang-related issues. So stop gambling before your head gets stomped.

Don't begin to gamble if you are not in a gang. The consequences for gambling if you are not a gang member can be extremely severe. Why? Because you are an island unto yourself, and you will not know who has been paid to settle the debt. Gambling has many ugly heads, such as card games, professional and college sports in addition to inmates competing against one another for pushups, pull-ups, fights, etc. Debts can be paid through commissary, specific requests (including sexual favors) or your meal(s). If you owe as little as $5.00, the debtor can pay $10.00 to have someone punish you. The lines in prison are long for inmates who can use $10.00. If you are expecting money in your account on Tuesday and funds are not credited to your account that day, your debt could increase by 100% per day. If the mail is delayed due to weekends or holidays; all the money you are expecting may be owed to your debtor. Failure to pay your gambling debts can get you killed, but so can paying late!

EPILOGUE

Throughout life, we're all confronted with those who choose to disregard the law, and, in ignorance of their circumstances, we falsely believe the same could never befall us. However, it's generally not until we find ourselves pressed against a wall or nearing the edge of despair that the possibility of crime as a way of life crosses our mind. Of course, other stimuli may be involved, but the message remains consistent: without first experiencing circumstances that might divert us from the high road, we can't know for certain that we'll never follow a darker path.

In reading these commandments, you've experienced to some degree how imprisonment (the eventual result of a life of crime) equates to an unconditional sacrifice of your current way of life. To anyone contemplating deviating from the high road or anyone currently in danger of finding him or herself under the radar of law enforcement, it's my hope that you take a moment, however brief, to reevaluate your perspective. Consider all that you have now and all that will be lost should you find yourself having to employ these prison commandments.

We are all the unfortunate children of a world where, very often, the true teacher is experience. Oftentimes, we find salvation in a kind gesture, a few stray words, the inking on a pamphlet, or code of a website. But how should we know that before us lies the answer to a question we've yet to ask: Is it worth it? These revelatory moments pass with such grace, with such unimposing haste that we might end up at a loss for time, unable to bask in those words of salvation long enough to grasp them. But here, if nothing else, see these texts for what they are: guidance.

If you, dear reader, are still attending school, know that imprisonment may send askew the entire road ahead of you.

Perhaps you are an exceptionally gifted athlete, stock broker, entertainer, politician, and attorney or business person.

What today is a perversion of rationality shall become your actuality, a prison— both literal and metaphorical—that will rattle the very foundation of your life. If you have surpassed those moments of childhood and are fully formed, the repercussions of your actions need not be reiterated. However, this isn't to deter you from the message herein contained. This is encouragement to rethink and reconsider any choices that might leave you at the mercy of the prison world described by these commandments. The threat to your future is very real. In the interest of preserving your way of life, I implore you to take into yourself this preventative information and embed it into your every action.

Wishing you the best,
John "Doc" Fuller

GLOSSARY OF PRISON TERMS

A

AB: Aryan Brotherhood.

Ad-Seg: Administrative segregation. When a prisoner is placed on Ad-seg, he or she is being investigated. He may have been involved with a fight or caught with contraband and go to the hole until the investigation is complete.

A Wake up: The day of an inmate's release.

All Day: A life sentence, as in "I'm doing all day."

All Day and a Night: Life without parole.

B

Back door parole: To die in prison.

Beating the gums: Inmate who talks a lot.

Bean Slot: In solitary/segregation cells, a place in the cell door where food trays are delivered or where an inmate places his or her hands for cuffing before the guards open the door.

Beef: A criminal charge, as in "I caught an armed robbery charge" or a problem with another inmate.

BGF: Black Guerilla Family (prison gang).

Blood: Primarily African American gang (Wears the color red with pride).
Bo-Bos: Tennis shoes issued by the prison system.

Book: Twenty postage stamps of the current first class value.

Books: Administratively controlled account ledger that lists each prisoner's account balance.

Bone Yard: Area where conjugal visits take place.

Brake fluid: Psychiatric meds.

Bug: A prison staff member considered untrustworthy or unreliable.

Bug juice: Intoxicants or depressant drugs.

Buck Rogers Time: A parole or release date so far away that it's difficult to imagine.

Buck Fifty: To get sliced across the face with a knife or razor blade.

Bullet: One year's time.

Bum Beef: A false accusation/charge or wrongful conviction.

Bum Rap: An unfair sentence.

Bunky: Cellmate.

Burrito Man: An inmate who has a hustle of making burritos for other inmates.

Buster: An inmate who is a fake or untrustworthy.

Bust Some Z's: A short sleep period such as a nap.

C

Cadillac: An inmate's bunk.

Cadillac Job: An easy or enjoyable inmate work assignment.

Care Package: Food or clothing sent from a friend or family member.

Cat Head: Hard rolls or biscuits served in the cafeteria.

Catch a ride: A request to a friend to get you high.

Cell Gangster: An inmate who puts on a tough front or runs his or her mouth when locked in his or her cell but is a coward when interacting with other prisoners in the open.

Cellie ("Celly"): The person with whom an inmate shares a cell.

Channel Check: Changing the television channel in the prison dorm .

Check: When one inmate scolds another who does not make a rebuttal. If this continues, the person scolded is "in check."

Chin Check: To punch another inmate in the jaw to see if he'll fight back.

Chi-mo: Child-molester, "chester," "baby-raper," "short-eyes," (as, "he has short-eyes," meaning he goes after young kids). The worst of all criminals in the eyes of convicts.

Check-in: Someone who has submitted to pressure, intimidation, debts, etc. and no longer feels secure in population and "checks in" to a Protective Custody (PC) unit .

Christmas Tree: A shank that is easy to push in but difficult to pull out.

Cowboy: A new correctional officer. Cowboy spelled backwards is "yobwoc" or a "young, obnoxious, boy we often con."

Contraband: Any item in an inmate's possession that the penal institution does not allow.

Convict: A longtime inmate, who plays by the "code" of prisoners, is tough, knows the ropes, and does not mislead or lie to other prisoners.

Crips: Primarily an African American gang (Wears the color blue with pride).

Crow: Lookout for other inmates committing crimes/rule infractions in a penal facility.

Cups on the Bar: Expression used by runners/orderlies in county jails that instructs inmates to put their coffee cups on the cell bar. Coffee will be poured in the cup when the runner/orderly passes by the cell. Inmates will not receive coffee if their cup is not sitting on the bar.

D

Dance on the blacktop: To get stabbed

Dap: A greeting between inmates by hitting the top of one inmate's fist with the bottom of another inmate's fist

Diesel Therapy: A lengthy bus trip or transfer to a faraway facility, or even an incorrect destination, used as punishment or to get rid of troublesome inmates (most often federal inmates)

DC Boys: A Washington, DC African-American prison gang.

De-Seg: Disciplinary Segregation. When an inmate is on De-seg, he or she is in the "hole" for an infraction.

Dime: A ten-year sentence.

Ding Wing: A prison's psychiatric unit.

Dipping in the Kool Aid: Jumping in another person's conversation. Being nosey.

Down: The amount of time an inmate has been incarcerated.

Drive By: When an inmate or C/O walks by a bed or cell while passing gas.

Driveway: Front of either a cell or a bunk.

Double Up: To charge double the principle for a late payment on a drug debt.

Dry Snitching: To inform on another inmate indirectly by talking loudly about their actions, behaving suspiciously in front of correctional officers, or supplying general information to officers without naming names.

Duck: A correctional officer who reveals information about other officers or prison staff to inmates.

Dungeon: Solitary confinement or De-Seg cell where an inmate is kept incarcerated as a disciplinary action for a violation of the institution's rules.

E

Ear Hustling: Trying to listen in on another person's conversation.

Erasers: Processed chicken chunks commonly used in prison food.

F

Fire on the Line: A warning by other inmates indicating that a correctional officer is in the area.

Farmero: Spanish slang for a Nuestra Familia member

Fish: New inmate.

Fish Kit: New inmates blanket, bedroll, sheets, etc.

Fish Tank: Intake Center for a prison

Flick: Picture from a magazine or a photograph.

Four piece or four-piece suit: A full set of restraints, composed of handcuffs, leg restraints and waist chain, and security boxes to cover the restraints' keyholes.

Free World: What inmates call the rest of the world outside of prison.

Fronting: Putting up a front about having lots of money, being tough, or having lots of women.

G

Gassing: Throwing feces at a guard or prison employee.

Get at: To reach out or contact another inmate.

Ghetto Penthouse: The top tier of a cellblock.

Good Time: Time or merit when a prisoner receives a reduction in sentence for following the prison rules. Federal inmates do not receive good time.

GP: General population in a prison. This is where the majority of the inmates are kept rather than solitary confinement.

Greener: Inmate who does not know about prison scams or stealing. Usually new to the prison system.

Gump: A homosexual.

Grandma's (Grandma's House): A prison gang's headquarters or meeting place, or the cell of the gang leader.

Green Light: To mark an entire gang for death. The green light can also be applied to single individuals.

H

Hack: A correctional officer.

Hats And Bats: Prison goon or riot squad. Generally called in to extract inmates from cells or stop a prison riot.

Heat Wave: The attention brought to a group of inmates by the action of one or a few, as in "Joe and John got caught with contraband, and now the whole tier is going through a heat wave."

High Class: Inmate who has Hepatitis C.

Hold your mud: To resist snitching at all costs.

Hole: An isolation ("segregation") cell, used as punishment for the most paltry of offenses as well as serious offenses.

Holla At Ya': I will talk to you later.

Hooch: Prison alcohol made by inmates. Contains sugar, yeast and generally orange juice, fruit from the cafeteria which has been cooking in a container or plastic bags for several days.

Hung up the gloves: To defect from a prison gang or organization by entering protective custody.

I

In the car: To scheme with another inmate on a deal.

Iron Pile: Weight, weightlifting equipment, a.k.a. "the scrap yard.

Institutionalized: Long-term inmate who has accepted prison as a way of life.

J

Jack Book: A magazine containing pictures of women.

Jacket: Prisoner's information file, also a prisoner's rap sheet or reputation.

Jacket: An inmate's information file or rap sheet.

Jack Mack: Canned mackerel or other fish available from the prison commissary. Can be used as currency with other inmates or placed in a sock and used as a weapon.

Jackrabbit Parole: To escape from a facility

Jigger: Lookout for other prisoners who are breaking prison rules, committing crimes.

Jockers: Aggressive inmates who use other inmates as their "prey."

Joint: Any prison or jail.

Joto: Spanish for homosexual or faggot

Jungle: The prison recreation yard.

Juice Card: An inmate's influence with guards or prisoners to accomplish goals .

K

Kite: A letter sent to a person on the outside or another inmate.

L

La Eme: Spanish for the letter "M." La Eme is the alternate name for the Mexican Mafia.

Legal Beagle: Inmate who works in the prison library. This inmate can be a law clerk or paralegal.

Lifer: An inmate who will never be released

Lock Down: When all inmates are locked in their cells due to an assault or escape

Lock in a sock: When locks and other contraband are placed in a sock and used as a weapon

Locker Knocker: An inmate who is marked as a thief.

M

Mail Call: Delivery of mail to prisoners.

Mail Out: A common practice in prison where drugs are given on credit or one owes money due to a gambling debt. The inmate owing must have his family or friend mail a money order to an address provided by the debtor. Payment must be made within two weeks or the debt doubles.

Med-Line: Medication or pill supply line within a prison.

Money: Postage stamps that are substituted for cash.

Monkey Mouth: A prisoner who goes on and on about nothing.

Monster: HIV. Also known as "the Ninja".

N

Newjack: Corrections officer or guard who is new to the job

Nickel: Served a prison sentence of five years

Ninja Turtles: Guards dressed in full riot gear. Also known as "hats and bats."

Nazi Low Riders (NLR): A white supremacist prison gang

No Smoke: To follow staff's orders without resisting or causing any problems.

O

Old School: Reference to the way prisons and inmates used to be. He can see a lot but say little. He can make a deal with a handshake. Often they are respected among officers and inmates.

On Vacation: When an inmate has been placed in solitary confinement

Orderly: An inmate whose job is to maintain the cleanliness of the housing unit

OTC: Out to court

Out-count: To count an inmate whose whereabouts are accounted for but not in his/her assigned cell

O

Out of Bounds: Any area inmates are not allowed.

P

Packing the rabbit: Inserting contraband into a body cavity

PC: Protective Custody

PC Up: To enter into protective custody. Generally for sexual offenders or weak inmates.

Peckerwood: Usually used by Blacks to describe white inmates

Peels: The orange jumpsuit uniforms worn by prisoners in some facilities

Pepsi Generation: Newer, younger prisoners, who lack respect for Old School ways.

PO: Parole officer.

Police: Corrections officer, guard, or staff of a federal prison facility.

Popped: An inmate that has been caught with contraband.

Prison Wolf: An inmate who is normally straight on "the outside," but engages in sexual activity with men while incarcerated.

Public Pretender: Public defender. Most inmates do not consider public defenders to be good at their job.

Punk: Term for either a homosexual inmate or a weaker inmate who performs as a homosexual for protection.

R

Rat: An inmate who informs on other inmates to corrections officers. Can also be called snitch or stool pigeon.

Rabbit: An inmate who has a history of escape attempts or has plans to try to escape.

Regulate: A beating administered by 13 Sureños for 13 seconds. Sureños is an organization of different Hispanic street gangs.

Resident: A Hispanic inmate who is not a gang member but still supports Sureño racial violence.

Ride with: To do favors for a fellow convict, often sexual ones, in exchange for protection, contraband, prison currency, or commissary items.

Ride Leg: To be friendly with or suck up to staff in order to get favors.

Road Kill: Cigarette butts picked up from roadsides by prison work crew. They're brought back to the facility and the collected tobacco is rerolled with toilet paper to smoke.

Robocop: Guard or corrections officer who writes inmates up for any rule infraction possible. A helicopter used to track a person running from law enforcement.

Rod: A prison stabbing device similar to an ice pick.

Rolled it up: A phrase used to describe an inmate who has entered into protective custody.

Rollie: Inmate's handmade cigarette.

Running Wild: Inmate who has a longer time in prison because he must serve consecutive sentences rather than serve all of them at the same time.

Run a Make: To locate and check the credentials of an inmate to see if he's an informant.

Runner: A person who does favors for prisoners, such as smuggling drugs into the institution, relaying messages, etc.

S

Sally Port: Secured control area where inmates/guards enter a jail/prison. Can be between two fences or doors

Sandwich: To stab an individual using two or more assailants, thereby sandwiching the target

Scam: A hustle or scheme to obtain something.

Scandalous: Can be either unbelievable or so outrageous as to be considered cool or okay.

Score: What an inmate obtained from committing a crime.

Screw: Guard or correctional officer of a prison.

Script: Money. Note: In many prisons, stamps are also used as money.

Scroll: A contract by an inmate to get someone.

Segregation: Usually SHU or another part of prison where inmates are kept away from the main population and most privileges are taken away.

Send-Out: Any monetary transaction in prison where an inmate gets another inmate to make the payment.

Shake Down: Search by guards/corrections officers of inmate areas for contraband.

Shank: Any object an inmate has made into a knife/shiv/sharpened point.

Short: An inmate whose sentence is less than two years or as low as imminent release.

Short Line: Line for prison store (commissary) during lunch hours or early lunch for inmates with medical problems.

Short Timer: Inmate who will soon be released.

Shot: In federal prison, this is an incident report filed against an inmate.

Shot Caller: An inmate who represents and speaks for a group within the prison such as a gang, dorm, or racial group.

SHU: Secure Housing Unit where problem inmates, such as gang leaders and those who are disruptive, are contained and privileges are mostly suspended.

Sick Call: An inmate visiting the medical section of the prison whether for illness, questions, or an appointment.

Slammed: An inmate who has been put in solitary confinement or administrative segregation.

Sleeved: Any person who has tattoos covering the entire length of his or her arms.

Sleeves: Any person who has tattoos from their neck to the wrists.

Snitch: Inmate who informs police, prison officials or authorities about rule breaking by others for a shorter sentence or favors. Also known as a squealer or rat.

Spook: In the federal prison system, staff who work in the Gang Intelligence Unit.

Stainless-Steel Ride: Death row inmate term for legal injection.

Screw: A correctional officer.

Self PC: To refuse to go to the yard or come out of your cell but not enter protective custody.

Shift Gears: To jerk a knife around in circular motions while it is embedded in the torso of the target in an effort to cause massive trauma and death.

Short: Close to a being released from prison.

Skinheads: A white supremacist group

Slocking: Using an inmate-made weapon consisting of a bag with a heavy object in it to hit another inmate.

Stainless Steel Ride: Death by lethal injection.

T

Take It To The Stall: Going to the shower area to physically settle disputes by fighting.

Tank: A dormitory unit within a prison consisting of 10–12 inmates. Contains both a day room and a bathroom.

Tats: An inmate's tattoos.

Ten-Minute Move: Moving between locations within a prison. These times begin at five minutes before the hour and end at five minutes after the hour.

Three Knee Deep: To stab someone so that he or she is injured but not killed, usually as a warning.

Throw down: A fight between inmates.

Tio: Spanish for "uncle." Tio is often used in prison and jail correspondence to indicate that the person being called "tio" is in fact a Mafia member.

To have the keys: To be in a position of leadership.

Tomahawk: A jail/prison manufactured slashing type weapon constructed from razor blades and melted plastic stock.

Two For One: A common practice in prison where drugs are provided on credit with the expectancy that the principle debt will be paid back double the value of the drugs.

Toss Salad: To sexually turn out another inmate by performing oral sex on their anal area.

Turf: Gang territory.

Turn Out: To force an individual into homosexual activity.

Turn: To cooperate with law enforcement.

U

U A: A urinalysis test for drugs.

UBN: United Blood Nation, an African-American prison gang (Wears red with pride).

W

Wacked: High on drugs.

Walk In: To allow membership into a gang without initiation.

Walk the line: To be an inmate on the general prison population.

Wearing the brand: Wearing a gang's tattoo.

Wolf Tickets: To talk tough or challenge others, without any intent to back it up with action or violence.

Y

Yard: The recreation area within the prison.

Yard-In: The command guards or correctional officers give at the closing of the recreation yard.

Yard-Out: Announcement that lets inmates know they can go out to the recreation yard.

Yolked: An inmate who is muscular.

Z

Zapato: Spanish for "shoe." Zapato is a slang term used to describe the "SHU" or Security/Segregated Housing Unit.